Also by J. Wilder-Hall

Fiction

What Could We Have Possibly Known About Love Then?

The History of the World

The History of the World

Love Poems and Other Stories
An American Debut
Vol. 1

J. Wilder-Hall

for my parents

This book is a work of fiction. Names, characters, places, and incidents either are the product of the author's imagination or are used fictitiously. Any resemblance to actual persons, living or dead, businesses, events, or locales is entirely coincidental.

THIS IS A THOMPSON WOODS BOOK

For information, address Thompson Woods Publishing, PO Box 676, Fairfield, CT 06824

Printed in the United States of America

ISBN 978-1-7342383-2-7 (pbk.)

Book jacket and design by L.R. Pilotti

CONTENTS

THREE

AND THEN THERE WERE TWO

ABOUT THE AUTHOR

ALSO BY J. WILDER-HALL

The History of the World

In the Beginning

SALVADOR SANCHEZ (671 ATLANTIC AVENUE)

…and he said it was the same everywhere, that he'd traveled the world far and wide just like I wanted, just like I'd suggested, and yet in all that time nothing seemed to change.

I love you, he said.
You are my heart.
You give me hope, he said.
You are everything to me!

And I told him he was wrong. I told him I didn't believe it—

1.

Having given the young beautiful waitress named Kimberly, who was originally from Hoboken, New Jersey, she said, a rather wan flaccid smile the one boy admitted with such listless appeal that he was so hopelessly in love with the other girl that he hardly knew what to do with himself anymore. The one great love of his life had vanished, promising never to return! At the bar we tried to cheer him up. But he was so insistent, drunk and apparently maligned that with hardly any provocation at all he suddenly began talking in hushed strained garbled tones about cashing it in at one point. Going so far as to exit the side door "much too early" – it hadn't even turned nine o'clock yet – (without telling anyone, of course, holding his sides in agony perhaps, perhaps crying! someone postured; and naturally in the grand hopes of escaping) as the band continued to play on *loudly* and a lone male baritone voice shouted above the mass hysteria reverberating underfoot while we all piled close to that second-floor window to see…laughing heartily, I must admit, and then screaming obscenities in his general direction as the rain started to pour down in sheets, the earth quake and the long tanned body of that enormously sullen young man and former high school track star (our hero!) grew smaller and smaller. Later, after he fell from sight, we returned to the bar, ordered drinks and toasted that miserable son of a bitch. *How could we not?* We'd all been such good friends that summer…and in a way our lives just as miraculous. Glorious, we knew—*even then!* (and in no small part due that rather horrible, unexplainable tragedy which had befallen the other boy's sister several years earlier and was by no means easily dismissed). And yet so fleeting.

2.

—Talk to me, she said.
—No, he said.
—Put down your hands, and tell me what you're feeling.

3.

Imagine if it was polite to talk about God. If life could be more than they led us on to believe. Countless hours we might spend in the innocent suffocation of youth. Praising idle on our backs…we walk the length of beaches at twilight.

Act One

Look. I am nothing. (I admit it!)

"I fail even these stars which wash over my eyes."

PASODOBLE

A wind came through and raised her skirt up.
She pressed her knees together and blushed—
but only slightly. Laughing, she withdrew
the chair from the table, sat down
and removed a cigarette from her purse.

So what do you want to do? she said.
Where's Jack? I said as she looked at me
and I leaned forward to give her a light.

Just then the wind picked up. It was like
this great call from somewhere. *Sue was gone.*
I knew that now. And for a while we just held on laughing,
burning through an entire book of matches
as she drew on her cigarette hopelessly.
Crossing one leg over the other in vain.

HOW IT LEAVES US

I tell her what it feels like
to be perfectly still.
And how that makes the heart beat.
What quiet sounds like late at night
as cars race up and down the road
outside my bedroom window.
I say: Yesterday, I was sitting at the beach alone
and there were all these people around me.
And I was reading his poetry and weeping.

We drink our coffee and she tells me
she doesn't like it here anymore.
She says at one time she thought: yes.
But now she thinks: no.
The door swings open. A young couple walks in…
along with the cool September air.
Later, she says, And isn't this true? Sometimes
we just spend the rest of our lives searching.
And then it is gone.

ABRAHAM'S DESCENDANTS

1.

It is only the heart that becomes the heart that creates the life
that becomes the breath.

2.

What if God and the Devil had not imposed their will
on faithful Job?

3.

How else would the man have possibly known
how lucky they were
to be in love
all those years
despite the rain?

HUMAN NATURE

After noting perhaps the obvious,
I wondered what he could have possibly been thinking
before he jumped into the tiger's den and approached.
Someone said he'd mentioned the word *destiny*.
While, at the court hearing,
the man begged for mercy and forgiveness.
Crying and thanking the guards
for their role in preserving
his life with their guns.
The tiger doing the only thing he'd been given.

EASTON BEACH ENTRIES

September's leaf
turns, and the world on and on.

*

Silence trumpets
a voice swallowed by rain.

*

We live to die *only* to live again.

*

May winter's breach
suggest the world was here
when first I saw you.

"And it was only then, my dear, my heart! my fire, my life, my love! (and within the generalized sense of anesthetized madness) that he was able to make out the fury of sound which by all accounts had gone virtually undetected."

I don't like that bastard
that bastard is no good
I don't like that bastard one bit
do you know that bastard?
Arthur said

that bastard told me to get the hell out of here, go away
to get the hell off of his front steps, leave
as though I was doing something
but what was I doing?
I wasn't doing anything
you know what I mean friend?

what was I doing?
I wasn't doing anything

but that bastard doesn't like me
that bastard doesn't like us
you'd think he would
you'd think he'd like guys like you and me

(always smiling
smiling and shaking hands
talking this way and that way—
but what does it mean?
it doesn't mean a damn thing)

that bastard doesn't give a damn about people like us—
ordinary people
people just trying to get along
what does he care about people like us for?

8

we're not big money guys
what money do we have?
we're not big money guys
we're just ordinary people

if we were big money guys
we could live on those steps for Christ's sake
hell we could camp out if we wanted to
have a picnic with dancing girls *shit*—

continued from the previous page

but try doing it friend with ordinary guys like you and me
and that bastard isn't having it

I'm going to call the cops that bastard told me
if you don't leave the premises
get the hell off these steps here
I'm going to call the cops

go ahead I told him
call the cops I said
call everybody you want
I'm going to call your boss
how's that father?
I'm going to call your boss
as soon as I get out of here
"I'm going to call God"

2.

—Are you listening to me?! I hope you're fucking listening to me!
—What's that? I said. I'm sorry. Excuse me!
and proceeded quickly toward the door.

3.

...but don't you think he was scared,
Arthur laughed (and wiped dubiously, I noted,
at his filthy chin with plump alcoholic fingers)

don't you think he was scared one bit...

BOOKENDS

from the morning here
cars steer west toward the highway

until times appear in late afternoon

to head east a short bend
and are gone again

HEADING HOME: AND WITH THESE RAINS I AM FLOODED BY WORDS

That young turkey
with the crooked leg
the one I thought
was a goner for sure
limping around university grounds
that winter my wife went away

I saw again in reflection
now these winters have passed
limping upon a crooked leg still

that turkey dressed
in brillo beard and barreled belly
and feathers brusque brown
fanned at me an impromptu and "entirely belligerent"?
warning (You son of a bitch! I thought—)
as the bells from the chapel tolled
and I approached.

FOR THE LIGHT THAT HAPPENED THEN. AND THE REFRACTION NOW.

Having come all this way
only to realize
what has not been done.
That failure is a marriage
beyond the island of a single heart.
No one goes unscathed,
and there is no clear map
for this type of living.
We get to the story of our lives endlessly
by forging beyond the altar
and the limited capacity
of what even Christ alone can offer.
Love confuses.
But augments a music
that cannot otherwise be heard.
We must meditate upon faith always,
and allow our dreams
to become trampled daily
by wild horses.

THREE YOUNG WOMEN ON A TRAMPOLINE
Or What Remains Somewhere between Adolescence and Adulthood

All his life he'd dreamed about something like this.
Nights spent in his bedroom naturally as a young man
imagining such a scenario. But who could he tell this to?
He thought: Who would understand him properly?
He was walking his dog, he'd feel inclined to say.
Working through another poem.
Of course lost in his own head.
When suddenly the sounds of incredible joy.
Like nothing he'd heard in a long time.
A high shriek. Then moments later
the one girl asking the other for the bottle of soap.
All he could see was flesh, he'd explain, nothing more,
as he'd hurried past a small clearing out front
between the large rhododendron and the blossoming
crab apple trees and continued down the road.
Turning once, he'd admit finally (to a group of unsuspecting confidantes in line
at the local delicatessen the following morning,
but only once—)
when he thought he heard someone calling his name.

JULY FOURTH
for my father

Look at him. Look at him standing there
with his chest all puffed out. His arms crossed.
A pack of cigarettes rolled in his sleeve.
Who does he think he is leaning against
that old Indian motorcycle
in the photograph of himself just before the war.
Undoubtedly pretending for my mother's sake.
For his mother's sake. This wouldn't be the first time
his pale blue eyes gave him away.
His long hair and shaggy beard as though
he wasn't like his father at all.
Who (in the family photograph they kept
above the fireplace all those years) seemed dead
long before he became an old man.

FIRST TIMES (GROWING OLD IN A SMALL UNIVERSITY TOWN)

The boy wanders the fields
beneath the hot August sun.
Sees the ferry below.
And leaves markers along the way.
The spirit ranges as the heart yearns,
they'd warned. But, in his haste,
the boy dismisses the coloring for the leaf.
The lush green valley changing
from something it was not.
Arrival confuses miracle for wonder.
Innocence for the rest of that form.
Time begins its slow compromise.
The way back now hidden
and gone forever – "like ghosts of failed love
and relics from some impossible dream…"
The smell of his body

                    *

and soft curious lips. The terrible and awkward way
he went about the rest of it!
Outside the world was continuing
and I slipped further and further away.
The heart hesitates, I thought, resolves
and moves on.

The sounds of ancient footsteps returning,
I sat there with her first collection
of happy poems in the near dark.

The wild fantasies of a young man once—
I stared at the back cover…
wondering how someone so beautiful
could bear such pain.

I am a flower (she told me once)
forever decaying with the bloom.

And therefore

UNDERSTANDING

If God is a merciful god,
why should we wrestle our lives in periods,
restlessly washing ten years
at a single glance
trying to understand
what has come and gone.

If certainly at times
in His immeasurable love,
He shields us from life
to insist on life,

why burden the human heart
with thoughts of what might have been.
Or carelessly lament
what we wholeheartedly believed
those nights we gave ourselves to them
so freely.

WAR AND PEACE
In memory of Jack Gilbert

He said he knew he was finished
as soon as he'd come to it, as though
each of those poems or psalms rang out
like a chorus of a hundred tiny voices
signaling finally it was time to move on.
The spirit that longed to dance. Lost and alone
in that vast wilderness. Hungry and cold.
And finding it night after night
amid all that failing and ruin. How many years
a man can sacrifice between visions
and passions. Between meditations.
And the flux upon which our faith is founded.
Mighty rivers forged of steel.
Impenetrable rivets of God and darkness.
Mercy. Light. And everywhere stone.
The giant girders of a former Pittsburgh
whispered softly into a child's ear.
Sturdy and obstinate. Baffled by the pleasure
it could bring. Like casualties helping
each other, he wrote. In that unabashedly
happier time of day. Carrying her pale body back
to the place where she was going.

WHEN SHE SHOWED HIM THE PHOTOGRAPHS OF HER FROM THIRTY YEARS EARLIER, THEY CHOSE TO TALK ABOUT THE FLYING BIRDS IN THAT ROMAN PIAZZA

When I was a young boy there was a man who rode
an old Schwinn bicycle up and down the main street
singing merrily to himself. Weaving in and out of traffic
while the older boys outside the bar saluted,
and he rang his tiny bell. No one was interested
in talking about the broken tables and chairs
that were piling up around his house that summer.
Or the time he was standing in the middle of the road.
Crying and naked as the rain poured down in sheets,
and the police came to take him away.
Everyone called him "the mayor." Maybe because it is easier
to explain what has not been lost somehow.
Like building one basilica alongside another
in that sinking North American city, and yet refusing
to address the failing religion of man.
"Hearts and minds," they were instructed.
"Hearts and minds…" But when the smoke cleared, he said,
there was nothing but levels of mass confusion.
Along the banks of the Dnieper River,
four priests stand on thick blocks of ice amid the fire and fury
of a divided nation. In nothing but a black cloak and miter
the one priest hoists a metal cross as high as possible –
"Are you listening to me?! I hope you're fucking listening
to me!" *as some final plea for the defense* – as perhaps
the only thing that remained between them yet.
Hoping, by God, it would be good enough.

LAUDS

Whenever
at dusk
wild turkeys
on my front
lawn
taking off
for trees
beyond
my neighbor's house
is
a perfect
example.

THE NARRATIVE OF OUR LIVES

Because our lives are infinitely temporary
there is no reason to forsake happiness anymore.
Knowing the buildings we erect in good faith today
will be torn down equally by someone else tomorrow
allows us to live with greed in the clear presence of joy.
There is no greater burden we may impose
than believing who we are is somehow beyond
the language that binds us all together.
We cast our nets. Go step by step across a vast land.
While the trumpets of Jericho toll somewhere else,
may our trains creep steadily forward
as a hundred burning lamps surging brightly at noon.

"…And though she really wanted to believe him, she said, she really did, having awoken now in the middle of the night! she couldn't help but question the limits of his dream—"

SUMMER REQUIEM (TRYING BUT FAILING)
for Jean

The poem slips away and suddenly this
darkness the winds stir and I dream
of you tonight my love I will lie in bed
remembering the great caravan of cars:
the ones who arrived those summer
nights so early their headlights blazing
the others who refused to leave.

THE ROMANTIC HEART

What is it we lose most of all
when the cold damp winter winds
intercede too many nights in a row?

He said, "It is not so much
the full radiance of their light
we work to remember.

But the light itself
that great absence
finds difficult to explain."

BURDEN OF PROOF
August & Everything After

More than anything he'd wanted to understand God
in some tenable way.
And what he could make of the great mysteries.
Always there was that thing with his father too.
His mother coming in the middle of them several times,
insisting: What you don't like about each other,
you don't like about yourselves. When he was a teenager
he'd lock himself in his room for hours,
reading Plato, Emerson, Whitman and Thoreau.
For a time listening to nothing but *Astral Weeks,*
and refusing to talk with anyone.
His father growing more and more agitated that night
he stared into his dinner plate with hardly the energy to eat...
(It had been a long time coming, that was for sure!)
Trying to recall every detail of that young woman's face
and the curious way she seemed to wave at him
when he was walking by.

Sue, what was it that kept us in that dark house
all those years? Was it love? Was it fear?
Was it the wild dreams of children
we still held onto?

POSTCARDS

And so
they excavated
the ancient mount,
hoping to find
eight civilizations
built on stone.
But the carbon debris
proved nothing new
in the end.
The language which occupied
the underground tunnel
showed joy while it lasted.
All along the city
were vestiges
of the dead...

THE FEELING OF THE UNEXPLORED

When she told me what'd happened
with her sons when she was away,
I said, Now there's a story for you.

And you should write it, she said.
I'm sure you'd tell it better than me.

We laughed, and I took in her sad eyes.
Her sensuous lips and high breasts.

I mean it, she said. I really do.
The small diamond on her ring finger,
projecting as much light as possible.

FOR A HUNDRED YEARS THERE WAS THIS SINGING

We manage the hours by guile and instinct.
By brash courage and faith. Belief and remedy.
We insist on life because we must.
Even as the relationship fails
and the words naturally erode.
She was the most beautiful woman in the world,
they say. The belle of the county.
No one within a thousand miles
was as exciting and full of life.
You should have seen her, the old men suggest.
The way she would carry on.
Stopping traffic and breaking hearts
like no one had ever done before.
The boy turns his head from the television
and looks indifferently at the old magazine covers
and the black and white photographs
from when they were young and in grade school together.
You have to understand, the women go on explaining.
Times were different then. We were different.
It wasn't like you people have it today.
What did we know about great romance. Fancy cars.
Traveling halfway around the world at a moment's notice.
We were the sons and daughters of a lost era.
Men and women determined to build a great nation
and fighting for it every square inch along the way.
An island of villagers left mostly to our own,
we were trapped within the small crowded spaces
of what we were trying so desperately to become.

FOUNDATIONS OF FAITH

1.

He opened the door only to find another door.
At the end of a long hallway,
he could hear the voices of children calling
and the rush of a train hurtling by.

He could not have understood what that meant
and was reasonable, they said afterward,
to stand there a moment in awe
as the doors fell suddenly open
and the long arms of their enormous shadows
withdrew ten steps to reveal the grand terrace
amid the music playing still
in the lush garden plaza
below—

where the news that had carried their names
fell gently
on the place
where it had gone down

2.

—"And so," she said, clicking her heels back and forth. "If it wasn't for sorrow how would we properly measure joy?" Closing the Tolstoy novel and now totally naked except for the large diamond ring, "If not for darkness, who would bear the heft of these stars…"

—"What about your husband?" I asked her.

—"What about him?" she said.

3.

you see the more we fight to live the more we find out we weren't the only ones after the afterlife *and then, after the show has ended, the floors swept, the linens folded, and the tables cleared and rolled away* may the judicious hand of a loving God find in this humble heart the seeds of His westerly wind—

first born of light, then temporarily blinded,
then black and white, then shades of grey.

GRAND CENTRAL TERMINAL
for Beth

As we moved toward the light
through long narrow corridors
of the city's subway station
there was filth everywhere
underground despair
broken dreams
a black woman shouting
Jesus Saves
to the rhythm of drums beaten
faintly at first then growing
louder and louder, *my dear*

CRESCENDO

Impressed
your
body
against
mine
and
for
a
time
the
mad
drum
beats
of war my love! my love! my love! my love! (beneath which
this
wild
heart
our
sea
winds
space
these
golden
leaves
through
sunlight
glows)

"And it was then, he knew, they were a long way from home!"

PERFECT STRANGERS

He tells me he has this recurring dream
about his aunt's house in Pittsburgh.
Which is odd, he admits, in a way,
not having been there in years,
not since he was a little boy,
what the mind chooses to remember.
Always, in the dream, he says
he stands in the middle of the road.
And it's grey out. Misty.
If you can imagine: that time of misty rain.
And I don't know what I'm doing there,
of course. You never do.
And part of me is scared. Part of me wants to leave.
And maybe I can feel myself starting to.
He looks at me and smiles his yellow teeth.
Laughs oddly as he raises his coffee
and leans back in his chair. I do not know
this man really. I don't even know his name.
It's strange, isn't it? he continues, and frightening
but so beautiful in a way. To wake up finally
and find yourself wanting to go back there
but never being able to for as much as you try.

LANGUAGE

When darkness comes,
even the flicker from a candle burns bright.

What most often we define as ending
is more clearly great arrival,

marking our long tender journey back

to the very root
of its beginning.

THE PERFECTION IN NOT FINDING IT

It was when he tripped over the long black robe
that was too big for him to begin with (clumsily
spilling the wine and the communion as the
man and his young wife in the first pew laughed)
that he should have known better. Which
is the same reason why April changes eventually,
and the favorite poet dies. Or is unable
to recognize his own words in the end
while the convocation gathers, and the one writer
interrupts to explain how the man's work had saved him
when he could not find his way out of a dark stairwell
alone. It is why people say everything that happens
happens the way it is supposed to whether we
can make sense of it or not. How that summer
they worked the horrible job for his brother,
digging up stumps until their bodies were nearly ruined,
they'd fish all night beneath a million stars.
Talking about the girls they loved.
Dreaming of their future lives.

YOUNG LOVE (AND THEREFORE)

Having just some hundred years, she said,
who were we to know it right away?
So we begged, *naturally,*
borrowed and stole.
Sometimes even cheated, sure.
But we weren't looking to hurt nobody.
We weren't trying to cause no harm.
Mostly he'd come up alongside me.
Always trying to show off or something!
Come up with these big protective arms:
Are you ready for something to believe in?
I swear: You should have seen the two of us go.
We'd get that old transistor radio to play
one of those long ago forgotten familiars.
And start dancing just like that.
In the middle of all them waste.
Telling each other things, the way he'd curl his lip
and then down below.
Going into the river and such,
and coming back again.
Staring at the rest of the world,
thinking like we'd be thinking.
His cowboy boots kicking up all that dust
and everything we'd go on meaning to do.
Like a million stars or something.
It was special—
Glimmering like people ought to be glimmering
out there in the middle of all that darkness.

WHAT WE TELL EACH OTHER SOMETIMES

Along the Midway
the shade is drawn—

the traffic stopped
and night comes on

for I didn't want
what I didn't have,

I only wanted
what I couldn't get.

And in the night
I shouted for you,

I shouted I shouted
the whole night through!

A FORMER LAND (WHEREIN MY DREAMS SHE
CALLS FROM AN OPEN WINDOW)

She remembers rats as big as dogs tearing through
the sewer pipes late at night when they were three
to a bed still *in order to keep warm.* Young girls
in their pretty flower dresses: eating peanut butter and jelly
sandwiches on white bread and laughing to themselves.
Those early winter mornings the old Grandpa cried and cried
as they lowered him drunkenly into the cold bath water.
What we are, she says, is doubled by a much larger faith.
When the light is cast high enough upon the sill, she can hear
the hurried sounds the forgotten men made in the back alleys
of immense stone churches wanting so desperately
to get it all down. Warm, lazy afternoons when her
brother found the neighbor's transistor radio to play,
and lines of soiled faces and former lands danced
all the way from the steel factories home.

THE TOUGH STEEL THE HUMAN HEART IS CAST

For twelve rounds they cheered
as the two Latin fighters
mauled each other in the center of the ring.
Heralded the sight
of blood spurting from their noses.
Round by round, the increased sound
of bones cracking sent legs quivering
beneath the full weight of ecstasy.
Later, out from the bar,
he goes home and fixes himself something to eat.
Hears the neighbors fighting again,
and sets down the knife.
Thinks about his own life. Things
he would have never imagined himself doing.
Things he hoped he would never do again.
But having done them *now* couldn't be quite so sure.
Remembering, at last, how beautiful she looked
the day they were married (as he
tunes the dial to hear the news
of that one fighter who was carried away).
How could anyone blame them, he tells himself.
How could anyone be angry with them at all
for believing the one thing they shared,
out of everything possible,
was some truly magnificent love.

STATIONS

what if god mattered, and the voices of children rang like a chorus of bells tolled from the courtyards each noon?

We were told to stand on opposite sides of the room.
Told it was all part of a much larger ceremony.
Jan's older sister Carol had the girls write their names
on torn pieces of paper while she looked for more
appropriate music, she said. And dimmed the lights.
Everything fell silent when Carol walked out –
holding the bright green bowl and asking for volunteers.
Some of the younger boys had older brothers and didn't
seem quite as nervous. When nobody came forward,
Carol's boyfriend Mike offered his services. If Carol
didn't mind, he said. Which made everyone laugh,
and mostly the girls. Tommy Hansen was the first
one of us to go…and I looked across the room at Melissa
trying to find the courage if the time ever came. Each couple
had two minutes, Carol instructed. And were told not to talk.
Everyone would get so embarrassed when Mike gave
his last-minute advice before closing the door. I remember
how large the room seemed at first. And dark. And the
small sound Donna made as I reached for her. Afterward
some people said they could smell the odor of the people
who'd gone there before. I didn't know and wondered
if that was true. As I looked across the room at Melissa
again. Who averted her eyes. And then back over
to where Donna had been standing.

NEVER BEING ABLE TO QUITE

None of it seemed right at the time
        but they told us to go along—

We were so tired by then anyway.
Death comes on easy
at a certain point.

HOUR BY HOUR: THE SELF-FINISHED EDGE

The seasons change
so that the body may follow.
The tides swell and generations
are beckoned forth to sea.
Always we should pray.
In life and in death.
Who else but a merciful father
would sacrifice his only son
and render us the handling of time
with diminished darkness
by starlight.

THE NOTES WITHIN THE MIDDLE PARTS

through fallen
snow

from driven rain

two-bundles
roofers

up again

past bend-in
ladders

with broken backs

and split-in
hands

toward midday sun (For I always wanted

to be something
in your eyes, he thought.

But when I failed

it was always her
who ran over

to see me.)

KNOWING WHAT WE'D HAD WAS TOO
DIFFICULT TO EVEN COMPARE

And yet

sometimes, she says,
shadows

on warm pavement
are just that.

God and rain
and the sudden rush

of wind
through tall trees.

As children we are taught
to believe
in the grandeur
of life.

But what are we to do,
if anything,

with the broken heart,
the darkened moon,

these adult memories
that flood
those shortening days
of two summers now

between us?

DUSK

When at last
he turned
to face the very thing
which had eluded him
so long,

was it himself he saw,
the manifestation of God,
or neither?

After a long day of writing,
I resign myself
to what remains—

and allow it
to wash over me
at last.

LOVE AND MARRIAGE

He pulls at the leash but the dog is stubborn.
"Come on," he says and the dog pulls back.
Baring his teeth, the whiteness of his snout
and back leg quivering in the full light of autumn.
The next morning one of the neighbors says:
My God, how much we were laughing,
my husband and I, watching the two of you.
We were having our afternoon snack, as usual,
when all of a sudden, there you were,
standing in the middle of the road,
arguing with each other. *You poor things!*
When you let go of the leash and shouted:
Well, if you want to go, then go, God damn it!
Leave! And the dog seemed unsure as to what
to do next. My husband said it reminded
him of an old story his father used to tell
of one married couple in particular
who'd been together far too long, and knew it.
But were simply too exhausted to do
anything about it now.

A LOVE POEM FOR THE INFIDELS

For in your great absence
these wild rivers run dry.

Such stars and moon
are cast to wind and rain.

And with these faceless people
move such faceless trains.

Whereupon rock becomes rock
set upon thicket and scorched land.

For in your great absence
these stomachs hunger legs and hands.

These love poems wander
from empty lips and eyes.

And all along the valley
there are only hills.

HOW THE WORDS SEEM TO FAIL EACH TIME I LOOK AT YOU

The body *then* torn and ragged,
my heart strained seemingly beyond repair
I stood at the mouth of the mighty river (four long years
grasping for the light switch in the dark)
when suddenly the sun rose, the birds sang
and everything became clear to me
all at once.

And what did you see, my love?

...for even the poet's words fall far too short
of what the child knew long before He
could
          utter a sound.

We use the blank spaces to hold what had happened there. Words are interchanged as history to explain what we know of the augmented heart. What penetrates is not the grand masterpiece as it hangs illuminated on the museum wall. Not the statue of Jesus bloodied and suffering in the old city alone. Not the light itself. Neither the poet amongst the living. But the body in transit for what it must necessarily become. The house burns down and is gone forever. Memories are ferried as misplaced stones. But the summer blazes to make something larger of the valley in the fall. The curtain closes, the stage runs black and the voices of the old-time singers croon on forever.

In scenes I write
By dimly light
In ageless couples
By painted moon
These stars and sun
These days in June

Whereon tireless eves
We go on cheek to cheek
Through hand in hand
By hip to hip, we sway—

Some perfect you
Cast perfect me
Whose hold on tight
And vanishing night

Not the Light Itself.
Neither the Poet amongst the Living.
William Doyle Kenney, 1973

Act Two

THE CONGREGATION THAT GATHERED THERE
BEYOND THE HILL WITH ITS BROAD STEPS
GOING DOWN

He stands there listening to the news: feeling empty,
feeling the sag of an entire nation. Problems everywhere,
it seems, he sits at his desk awhile and then stops.

Goes to the kitchen to make himself some tea,
and rubs his hands against the penetrating cold.
The psalms do not change. Only history is reformed.
The wooden cross is important because Jesus died for our sins
so we must find a way to give reverence for this kind of life.

He works well into the evening, crossing everything out.
Not the old stone church. Nor its stark white spire
reaching higher and higher still. But the chaste heart
which winds us small and small...Exhausted, he crawls
himself into bed, reads a few pages more and then stops.
Closes his eyes and continues that beautiful dream...

of the old Mexican couple in the yellow Datsun
from last summer...Cars flying past, they stood behind
the tall windows while the seven college students
ran from the café laughing to themselves.
"Because what else did they have to do?"

Five minutes later: the one girl
in the long flowered dress,
and no shoes.

Driving for the first time,
he could hear her say.

As the six aggressive boys
leaned their backs
into the trunk
of that ruined car.

And the old man
in the checkered shirt
ran across the street
directing traffic.

Smiling at the blonde wife,
who turned
a small delicate hand
just ahead
to the bright orange sign…

*It's like I tell everybody at some point. Gary had built
us a home in Galveston. A small house
that we'd made into a home…*

Looking back
occasionally
to wave

at those long slender bodies
drenched in warm sunlight.

*

*While overhead wild geese continue to trail westward—
so that twelve hours may begin
the long arduous flight home…*

ADULT DREAMS

maryann
this lifeguard stand

where we first kissed
like two drunk kids

now turned over
in winter display—

this bone cold wind
this haunting memory

BETWEEN MEN AND WOMEN (2)

She says she's worried about him. Says, Look at you.
You're so thin. You look like you're killing yourself.
Have you been eating? She says,
You don't look like you've been eating.
He tries to explain about the appetite. About fathers and sons.
But are you happy? she says. I'm worried you're not happy.
What Carver meant by *October* in the Photograph
of My Father in His Twenty-Second Year.
Gilbert, he says, not in quantity.
But in the size of that scale. Like Fitzgerald
believing himself a failure to the very end.
Hemingway, hungry and alone after the war,
walking the *Rue Denfert* with the statue of the two men
in flowing robes, and dreaming of lions
in the middle of a Paris summer.
As Abraham commanded Isaac, he says.
And the whole blessed covenant of Jerusalem because of it.
"But you're not making any sense," she says.
"Please," he says. "Can you hear yourself?"
"You have to try to see it from my point of view."
The man standing at the end of a long gravel road
twenty years after leaving the father behind.
First blinded by courage. And the eternal belief
of what could have happened there.

IN OUR TIME

at night on my drive home
beneath tall pole lights they line up their cones
one after the other for mile upon mile these men until dawn
when finally *my* shift begins and the cones are gone...

and these lines of brown brothers trucks
now parked as abandoned relics
along that familiar stretch of highway

WE GET TO THE SPIRIT BY HARD WORK

We get to the spirit by hard work.
By deliberate practice and arrangement.
By forging beyond the vague temperature
of what the heart already knows, we are seized
by the potential of the old wooden barge
heaped with trash as it moves slowly to the west
in the final moments of twilight. Getting smaller
and smaller, she said, we are sunlight crashing
as beautiful pools of sorrow and joy. A thousand
stars brilliant against the slate grey canvas God
also provides. Compliments to the grand overture,
we become the bright yellow leaves in the park
across the street from the church. Where the bells
toll and the elderly woman leans down pointing
at the newly married couple while whispering
into the young boy's ear. So that one day
when she is gone, he may properly understand
the higher measures of love and kindness.
The full extent of the young woman's beauty
as she lies in his bed covered in roses
but shivering from the cold. Joyful and crying
in their embrace. Hungry to bring him
that much closer.

THREE GENERATIONS OF LOVE STORIES

It's because you're young, she said,
and beautiful.
Young and beautiful?
It's because you haven't lived life
long enough to know.

The thin blonde woman rolled her eyes
and looked across the café
at the man in the buttoned shirt
and tan jacket.

Which reminds me of a story
my mother would tell,
the older woman continued
of the man who sold his house
to live with a colony of bears.

How happy they all seemed for a time,
and what a horrible tragedy
it truly was
the following spring

when the reporters returned
to interview the man
only to find
he'd already been eaten.

AGAINST ALL ODDS

Tenderly I arrive. Longingly I remain.
From beyond my neighbor's broken down porch
three small birds continue to sing—
and yet I wait for the one with its ruptured heart.
What a coup! Such poet's wind runs clear
straight through September's leaf this bright morning
all the way unto the following dawn.
I sit here in the darkness late at night
trying to capture the moon for I didn't see what I didn't hear
and I didn't hear what I didn't know

CAMELOT

He said it was because of the others that he didn't want to go there anymore. Everything had grown so old and stale by that point, and there was this feeling of never fitting in. Of having lived there his whole life and often talking about wearing a dress for the hell of it, and maybe that had been too long. With him going crazy and their incessant concern for things he didn't find all that important. Out of the whole bunch the only one he didn't mind was the old woman named Madeline, who'd come in around two after completing her shift at the bakery across the street. *And once claiming to be the lead dancer for the Eifman Ballet Company.* With us always at the bar and the two of them at the corner booth for hours, talking about her dream house overlooking the harbor and the young girls out front in their pretty dresses…and him always wanting to live like Hemingway. For a while, I remember, the great happiness from the leftover scones she'd bring, and the conversation and cheap drinking wine, while we all stood there watching and wondering. Her eyes glossing over that time he kneeled in front of her to remove her shoes. (That grand gesture which nearly floored us all!) Untying the laces first, and then gently running his hands along the splintered arches of her feet: knowing the pain that accompanied the struggle.

LOVE LETTERS

these are just some of the little things
she said
sitting in our old station wagon
that cold january afternoon
feeling
with her hand over my hand
the heat barely
trickling out
and check engine light
blinking on...
and seagulls
circling overhead
a plane off
in the distance
with smoke trailing
the final moments
of sunlight
beyond the old lighthouse
            but reaching still
toward the shore

where three or four couples
continued on
huddled close together
with water crashing at their feet
and wind whipping against their faces

PROMISES

All afternoon
the amount of snow falling
intensifies with the hour
and continuous drop in temperature.

The pole lights sputter
as the traffic lessens.

And I snap on this short table lamp
to the call of geese in nearby distance.

Prompting that old retriever
to turn his head
from some great elusive silence.

MEDITATIONS

Listening to the dark,
and the faint whispers beyond that.

       *

Writing happily awhile
(in the small barren room)

as light casts shadows
on the unknown page.

       *

Lifting my head
at the sound of music

and unmistakable joy.

       *

How the words seem to fail
each time I look at you.

NEWPORT, THAT SUMMER

I was lost that summer. What else is new?
Wanting to be a writer.
But knowing what was happening with my friends.
The amount of money they were making at their city jobs.
And me at the marina, knowing hardly anything about boats.
And, even worse, not caring.
The first one in my family to graduate from college.
And there I was, banished to the ice house
with a high school dropout named Eric.
All day shoveling ice into bags.
And hopelessly falling in love
with the young woman who lived downstairs from me.
That one party we had toward the end of August,
I thought it'd be romantic to get down on my knees
to explain where all of this was coming from.
A few minutes later everybody was looking at me
as her boyfriend walked out from the kitchen,
wanting to know what he'd missed,
what was so funny all of a sudden.
My heart turned over as I watched her disappear.
Her boyfriend pouring what was left of the rum,
I reached my hand out with the others.
Knowing now, I thought, what I needed to do,
what perhaps I should have done all along.
The ice continuing to melt in our glasses,
the summer gone, I was already beginning to regret it.

THE STORY OF CREATION BY GORDON LISH IN AN OPEN LETTER DATED JULY EIGHTH, 8 A.M.

What if having finished the galleys at last
and expressed them overnight with His blessing,
He suddenly received a wire in the mail
insisting—*by God!*—it was already too late?

      *

Homeless, gut-wrenched and poor, on the edge of something,
alone (but)

*Can you imagine spending the entire night / reworking these meager lines
as though there'd been some great merit / in preserving that lonely winter?*

MIRRORS

Oh, that was a wicked place, he said.
Cold and frightening and strange.
Certainly not the type of place a man goes
to raise a respectable family.
There were hookers everywhere. People poor
and hungry in the streets, making everything up.
Desperate to create a life as they went along.
You couldn't trust anybody, I'm afraid.
And least of all the beautiful girls.
Once when we were leaving the hotel,
three men with thick, aggressive accents rushed up
shouting *"the Americans, the Americans,"*
and damn near demanding a king's ransom for it. I'll tell you:
People thought we were crazy to go there in the first place—
and maybe we were. But who could have imagined the scale
of that Winter Palace at dawn? The sheer majesty
of her golden dome glimmering against the cold
as though God Himself had seized the opportunity?
When we came back, I kissed the ground
and swore I'd never forget. Which makes everything
that's happened since seem so incomprehensible now.

TEMPLATE

There is a time after the time after
we lay our warm bodies down

when our fingers form as hands
and our tongues turn as legs that

could wrap around the moon—
But oh how I love it *mostly* so

when in the cold dark winter's
night your eyes like great fires

drenched in rain roll like our
hips which drown out the sun.

SECOND CHANCES

Life's funny, Jack said.
The last year Maureen and I were together,
it wasn't that good between us.
It was awful really.
We argued a lot. We hardly made love.
And when we did make love,
mostly it was like making love to a corpse.
Which is worse than not making love at all.
Which is why when Maureen said
she was leaving, I was happy to get rid of her—
But now that she's gone.
And a few more years have passed.
And she's happily married with two kids
and a small Jack Russell terrier
she'd rescued from the pound...
I have fond memories of those days don't ask me to explain it
is it strange I know yes but then again what the fuck do you
want me to do? Especially when I find myself
in her neighborhood late at night.
Driving by her house.
And all the lights are off.

TEMPORARY FRIENDS

In the memory, at least,
we were better than that:
miles upon miles
of great daffodils in spring,
we'd rise out from the fog
untouchable.

GETTING READY

He'd lived there all but one year of his life. Fifty-three years,
we'd find out. And they spent nearly the entire time
we lived next door complaining about him. Screaming
about his laziness and the amount of food he consumed.
As he kept himself around the house in pajamas all day.
Or outside, in front, smoking one cigarette after the other.
At his funeral that fall someone said he died of a broken
heart several years ago. While a bald man carried a
black and white photograph from when they were just
fifteen years old to prove what a *tough tough* he was.
Look at the smile on his face, another kept saying.
While the two heavily rouged women sitting next to us
lamented how handsome he was before everything
had changed. A few weeks later we were standing
in the old couple's kitchen. Maryann said she felt funny.
But the old woman was so insistent that we decided
it was all we could do. "Eat, eat," the old woman would say.
"Please. Don't be shy. Eat, eat. Please help yourself."
And how happy it seemed to make her that none of the food
was going to waste. As we passed around heavy plates
of chicken and potatoes. Steak and lasagna.
And they alternated between wringing the mop
into the bucket the other held. "Eat, eat. Please.
We're not going to need it. Eat, eat. Please help yourself."
The old woman's voice growing more and more hoarse
as the afternoon wore on. Her husband appearing frail
and hunched over and shaking his head. Occasionally
stopping to remind us what a good son their child was.
Obedient and strong when he was younger. Good-looking.
A beautiful boy. And making the sign of the cross.
As our stomachs began to turn from all that food. And the old
woman continued to encourage us against what seemed
impossible. Tears streaming down both of their faces
at one point. The freezer continuing to defrost to the floor.

74

CALIFORNIA

How happy the young man looks now
chasing the dog who's dug at their flowers
and the young woman lying prone in the dirt
laughing and calling to them both.

BETWEEN MEN AND WOMEN

Mostly we want to get it right, he tells her.
To be kind and compassionate and brave.
Living our lives and doing the best we can
as human beings. But making mistakes
more often than we'd like to admit.
Finding ourselves sometimes desperately
searching as young boys still wild in the dark.
Pretending to know the higher order
of courage and strength amid their gentle
mouths and steady assurances.

—And so we fought for beauty, she said, and you push out the madness, and we drew our breath *naturally* again and again even if it was only for a few minutes at a time—

TUESDAY MORNING
for Peter

The storms moved in
and we were caught in the fields when it happened.
Racing out to the high grass at once,
knowing and yet not quite understanding
the nature of the subtle wind
as we held on close to the rails
to try to make it across.

AND YET ABOUT THIS POEM, MARYANN

isn't it true?
i could spend
the rest of my life
trying to make
it better

but the more we try
the more we seem
at times to foul up
something
that once was

THESE SAD FIGURES IN THE HISTORY OF LOVE

At least once an hour they would walk up to the room
with tall windows. It was so quiet that you could hear
their lavish voices ringing above the soft music.
Along with some wild story to tell of what had happened
there just a few days earlier. Always they appeared
so happy and young as they looked around at the rest of us
and stopped. When Dickens came to the place where
he had to kill off Little Nell (it's said) he walked
the streets of London with tears running down his face
until he went back inside and got it over with.
I returned to Rilke's elegies at once and tried to make sense
of the damned thing. Nearly out of money and waiting
(always waiting) — "like ghosts of failed love
and relics from some impossible dream…"
The smell of her body,

*

and soft curious lips. The devastating way
we went about the rest of it!

Looking at their skinny bodies I
imagined them later that night

parked at the end of some quiet road

(just like we'd been, maryann)

with the music turned low

catching their breath
against fogged windows.

CONDITIONS OF FAITH

He said it was good for a while. And then bad.
Good and bad: the way a marriage sometimes goes.
Wouldn't show any real interest in the things the rest of us
were doing unless it had something to do with the Church.
Or the steadfast principles of faith. Became a real bible
thumper once he got to the other side of drugs.
One of those refried Christians you read about.
Trading one addiction for another.
Always talking about our bodies as the grand temple.
And ingress to the Holy Spirit. How the past was the past,
and there's nothing in this world a man can do
but accept his fate going forward. We tried to show him
a good time. But he would hardly go anywhere
without keeping that bible handy.
Last month when the fellas were bored
and just looking to have an ounce of fun,
I kept thinking about that poem…
"We live our lives and dally in our dreams."
I wanted to remind him of God's enduring salvation for all.
But by that point there was nothing left to do
but get the hell out of his way.
When Jerry tried to give it back—
My God! how that boy nearly lost his mind.
Threatening to tear down the place with everyone in it
by what he found in those lost verses afterward.

NICK CARRAWAY ROAMING THE STREETS
OF NEW YORK CITY ALONE
for Estlin

How silly we are,
how silly we love,
how silly we fight,
how golden your hair,
how loving your lips
and silly these eyes
and perfect these hips
and rosy these thighs,
how searching these fingers
with silly this heart,
how golden the sun
how perfectly love.

HERE IS WHAT WE STILL BOTH HESITATE TO GIVE

All day he searches for it. In crowds
of coffee shops. On city streets.
In shadows that wave along a gravel path.
Considers what Hemingway said about love. And Gilbert.
And Jeffers about contemplation.
Considers the sunlight against the rails.
The happy couples on either side falling into each other.
If he leaves now he should be there by tomorrow morning.
Continues along the platform remembering
how beautiful she looked when she came to him.
The sun shining on her tears.
The tears that ran along her face so freely.
Pain is merely light's refusal to overcome the darkness,
he tells himself as the train's whistle starts just beyond.
Growing closer and closer each time, he thinks.
He reaches into his pocket for the ticket,
then crouches a moment
to where a lone dandelion has pushed its way
through the hard concrete.

FRAGMENTS OF A DREAM
for Franz Wright

Lord, will I wake up tomorrow?

Marie says,
While you were sleeping I watched the sun crest
over the moon.

This heart is your heart, she also says.

The train was full of people I didn't know.

OF ALL THAT NOW REMAINS

I will dream of you at midnight.
I will dream of you through heavy wind and rain.
The fog cannot dismiss what the sun most clearly sees:
this heart is your heart
and these words mean nothing besides—
I will lay like those lovers last
always in the soft grass pretending:
this wind and heart (this mouth
and these lips) which carry your name.
Long after the time when our time is no longer given,
I will dream of you at midnight.

FROM THESE ETERNAL WATERS

Knowing little more than what the heart seems capable of,
the young woman unbuttons her blouse,
removes her bra,
and leans her body in a steady rhythm forward.
For months she heard all their advice.
But now the baby fusses and she sits right up.
Carries the boy, she hums the song she did not remember.
A kind of world. Just like her mother had.
Filling the words that seem to go.

SHE WILL RAISE ME IN A BED OF FLOWERS
for Jack

And what happens to the book
that is no longer printed—

And the man who spends his entire life
dreaming of another world?

MARRIAGE AND CHILDREN
for Charles Bukowski

Afterward they will tuck the boy into bed
knowing, for now, this is all they can do.

She will lean her long, thin body against
the boy's flushed cheeks. The young father

making quick work of the bedside table lamp.
"Close your eyes," she will insist of them

both. Recalling *a time* those great African
elephants circling the ring. And see them

standing there exalted. She'll say:
"See how much they like the sun."

All year he wades through forbidden depths of silence, burrows
himself within the brick and mortar of old sinking ships only to
manage joy from a small wooden spoon. How else could I
possibly explain this lonely vigil I keep, these failing words that
steal the page—night after night, it seemed, all last winter:
a single pair of deer tracks left ominously in the snow?

Knowing the Poetry Recedes
H.T. Woods, 1949

I was broken, he said.
Everything about me destroyed.
What else can a person say
to something like that?

My whole life *I gave myself*
to the possibility
that we would fall in love—
truly and forever.

But the fact of the matter is:
You take the light of God
that shines down
on a man his entire life.

The way their pretty eyes
can hold you mostly
through the dark.

The type of heart and yearning that entails
when we draw close
to the full range
of human experience.

Sometimes
when I consider
how magnificent
this life really is,

I could just about
curl up in a ball
and cry.

Act Three

BLACK AND WHITE AND SHADES OF GREY

Now there he is in a series of photographs.
And now my father handling the yard. All his life
insisting a man remain vibrantly strong.
When all I desired was eternal vulnerability.
Did you hear my cries? What is it
the obedient son learns from watching you? As here I gaze
at a young man just fifteen years old…My father,
before you wanted anything, what was it
you wanted most of all? Now, nearly forty, I remain.
Trying to arrange the pieces of this unfinished life.
Have I made you proud? What would your father think?
They said certainly *for a time* it was your mother's Alzheimer's
which drove you over the edge. Is it true
that often the human heart is forged in great tragedy?
What does the blind eye seldom see?
These mornings, by His own volition,
the sunlight enters our weary house. Scatters and is gone.
Lately, in each of these poems as I begin:
Your failing eyes loom heavily over my consciousness.

JANUARY 31, 2013

i listen to the morning news
i do not understand it
i drink my coffee and read
a story i've spent several
weeks on and get depressed

i call maryann
but she does not pick up the phone

my best friend's wife texts
where have you been?
we've missed you
btw—jack had surgery
did you know?

what for?
i respond

his nose—lol
he didn't like the look of it

(my god, could this possibly be true?)

i snap open the blinds
just beyond my desk
as three fire trucks
with their sirens going
tear down the street

and suddenly it is 2010
and we are having dinner
and something is said
and my ex-wife tosses
the salad bowl to the floor

then the rice, the chicken
the glasses, the utensils

and i work my hands
around her throat
and threaten to set
the whole goddamn place
on fire

the phone starts ringing
my whole body is shaking

i take a deep breath
and look at the number calling

hello, i'll say (good morning, she'll say—)

i was married in the midst
of an indian summer
today it's grey out
tomorrow
they're predicting snow

things are going to change
i can feel it.

OF SUNSET RISES AND MOMENTS LOST
FOREVER

the people we meet
on trains
those standing next to
on subways
within seas of city streets
out where no one is looking
to sounds of a countryside road—
where miles and miles of
tall trees converge
with evergreen
dusty plains
and asphalt drive
driven telephone poles—
when every so often
persists,
these light wind
heavy rains
and pale skies
the cloudy day,
to glimpse a line
of them
at the very top—
some simple birds
flying about
some simple birds
from north to south
upon simple cables
and small tree poles
streaming
who where when why
you ought to know—

beneath a pale blue
sky
on top of evergreen
plain,
some say

AS THE BUILDINGS OF OUR FORMER MASTERS ARE TORN DOWN

i.

If the story of our lives is meant no more or less
to drive down to the full range of human
experience and *burrow* there, why
should we delude our spirit
with visions of a self
contained world?

ii.

We look at the sun, believe
we can control the weather

because of what we track as a thousand years of progress

and a nation is
divided in two.

iii.

I remember as a young boy lying in an open field late at night:
leaves falling everywhere
as a line of geese flew overhead
all the way unto the following dawn.

iv.

If the language between us ceases to exist,
how shall we communicate
the depths of who we are?

v.

If we're afraid to say
God and family are all we have…
when everything else falls apart,
what will we do
with the rest
of it?

vi.

Yesterday, I was lost in the dreams of a young child
two stories up—
his blushed face pressed against the glass
of the tall windows looking down
at the main street below.

vii.

Maybe it's because the human heart triumphs
"against our insistence" (Maryann believed)
that we're able to stare beyond the ocean
as the barge moves slowly across…
trying to decide where one part
of our lives ends, and the other
begins.

US, AT THE COFFEE SHOP

us
at the coffee shop

us deep in thought

us regulars
—ten to twelve

us staring out windows

GERTRUDE STEIN TALKING TO JOHN DOS PASSOS ABOUT MATTERS OF SELF-PRESERVATION DURING THE GREATER PART OF THE TWENTIETH CENTURY

Don't do it, Jake! she begged. You don't have to.
How do you know?
Put it down, honey. Please! We'll be all right.

Always and again these stories of endless confusion.
A lifetime of drifting only to realize what has been there
all along. Like stacking stone upon stone needlessly
while a hundred bushels of light lay hidden at the entrance
to Enaim. A lot of very strange things happened there,
Gilbert said wide-eyed and laughing once. If you
really want to know. So maybe we have a chance after all.
The sun rises, sets. Then presses on to the place where it shall
be going. Soon after his great love for Hadley waned,
Hemingway compelled the ending to Catherine Barkley's life
more than forty times. Until there was nothing left to do,
he wrote. But shut the door and turn off the light.
Leave the hospital room at last and walk back in the rain.

JUST THEN, HOPEFULLY

And besides what kind of life did he have in the end (she said)
living with our parents still at more than fifty years old.
Naturally sick from a broken heart, and then finally
those last two years full of cancer. When he started
walking around the house late at night talking crazy,
I kept praying for everyone's sake he'd go peacefully in his
sleep. I mean, was I wrong? Tell me! Was I out of my mind?
Because I didn't know what else to do!
(I was so scared in the hospital room that time
the nurses left and he sat up in a rush grinning!)
What is it? I yelled. John, what do you see?
Afterward, everyone said he was in a much better place now.
But I wondered how could you be so sure? The other day
when I turned on the radio to clear my head, a breeze tore
through the kitchen window knocking the large glass vase
to the floor. A minute later *of course* I was on my hands and
knees: crying and laughing at the same time, cutting my fingers
on a million shards of glass, watching that old photograph
from when we were kids (and he was thin and handsome
and just months engaged to the beautiful woman)
pick up with speed in the increasing wind.

And so what happens to the book that is no longer printed? And the man who spends his entire life dreaming of another world—

LATE NOVEMBER IN A FIELD OF WHITE
CHRYSANTHEMUM

Where in the end I will go to sleep
amid the fields of black and white.
My father will be there—
I am sure of it. Slightly taller than the rest,
His pale blue eyes will illuminate the way.

JUST BEYOND THE GOLDEN BRIDGE FROM INLAND THAT HAS BROUGHT US HERE

He'd been a captain more than thirty years. Was big and burly.
But admitted (even he) the C-shaped marina, though beautiful,
was difficult to navigate at any age. It was my first (and only)
summer living in that remote seaport town,

and I'd just come down from the ice house
when he called me over to lend them a hand. Of course, I
tried to remind him of what had happened there the last time!
But he just threw me one of the ropes and laughed.

The young woman he called "the missus"
was going around the dock, crying and hugging everyone.
Blowing kisses and talking about the things they planned
on doing the following summer. I reached along the dock.
And she drew her arms around me at once (refusing to let go!)
until I promised to finish the book I'd been writing
by the time she returned.

Out of the corner of my eye I could see the owner's daughter
looking at me. While the captain gave the signal, and the rest
of the crew climbed to the prow of their small wooden boats
with long-handled brooms.

All I had to do, they said, was keep in front as best I could.
And not fall in. And for a while, I remember, there was
nothing but hollering back and forth when a first wave came.
And the boat swung to the right, almost hitting.

I pulled against the heavy rope at his command,
and the missus screamed out, "You'd better tell her!
You'd better tell her before it's too late!"

...How many times I've sat there hopelessly since trying to find the right words—

> We are born back ceaselessly from the ash.
> Catch our lives time and again.
> Sail our hearts on paper boats. Engulfed in fire.
> If we are lucky enough.

DREAMING OF LOVE

He said, I know it sounds crazy.

But sometimes lying in bed
with her sleeping soundly
beside me,

how much I long for those nights
before she'd come back...

When I was so pale and sick
and hoping to die.

And the world, in a way,
so full of possibility.

THOSE DAYS WERE AFTER ALL

there was sadness
everywhere
in the stories
they told
as they stared
at their phones
drank lattes
applied gloss
to their lips
shook their heads
and gasped
for emphasis

THE HISTORY OF THE WORLD (RETROSPECTIVE)
Love Poems and Other Stories

After all those years
I don't know why I didn't see him much then.
We were so close at one time that maybe
the reasons they give are not that far off.
Maybe this is truly all we have
in arriving at the end of something knowingly.

It's hard to say for sure what Sue was thinking,
whistling through the halls as we packed our things
to leave the house for good and go our separate ways.

Of course, it bothered me at the time. But thinking
back maybe it wasn't so strange after all
when she laid there gasping her final breaths,
and he lifted her shirt in the hospital room
and stood watching.

CONVERSATIONS CONTINUED FROM A PREVIOUS PAGE

—I love you, he said.
—I just don't know, she said.
—What don't you know? he said.
—Do you really love me? she said.

WISHING HER WELL (NOW FOUR YEARS LATER)

The seas change. Drift in and out. God holds His breath
taking everything back. Like the well-practiced poet
failing at the middle of his life. The long stretch
of November beach in front of him still, he continues
along without any more of the unnecessary delusions.
Happy enough to remember the boy who wandered
through the quiet New England town before dawn.
Bright red face from the stir of young love, he carried
the five-gallon pail up seven flights of stairs to the apartment
they'd rented at the corner of Eliot and Wafely Terrace
for three hundred and fifty a month. She'd been
in a dead sleep when he walked in and could not understand
what he meant by laying the three fish on the bed at once,
and showing them side by side. Feeling foolish even then
to sit in the cold temperatures of that early spring morning
wondering what he should do now that he let the fish go.
Content to watch the sun rise across the increasing distance
between them. The long reach of God's mercy and grace
changing the colors from light to dark to light again.

      *

—In the absence of light we are the body without form
—A painting without color or movement the words get lost
from here to there...

—In Heaven they are the ones we hunger for always on those summer nights alone
— *"Dreaming of lions but realizing the moonlight at last"*

ACT I: ORIGIN OF ACTION, PART 1

...not to mention that whole shit with god and the goddamn history of the world—

What about God? What about the history of the world?

...they don't like you, Arthur said, don't you get it? how many times do I have to explain it to you? they don't like you one bit, don't think they do, don't you even think it, you're not their kind, you know, you know what your people say about them people, Arthur laughed

you know what I'm saying to you
you can't trust them people
them people are not to be trusted, no—
don't think you can
don't you even think it

let me tell you something, friend
I've known plenty of them people that will steal
your underwear in the broad daylight
beat the hell out of you and steal your underwear
that's what kind of people they are, mean—

mean mean people very mean
you can't trust them people
people are mean today, especially them people
them people are not to be trusted
but how do you know?

how do you know what people are thinking?
I don't know what *you're* thinking
how would I know?

you don't know what people have been through
what shapes people
how could you?

some people have had it hard,
harder than you could ever know, beaten—
beaten like goddamn animals, some people
beaten like dogs
beaten by their own parents even
beaten from head to toe and left for dead

and then *some* people start wondering why *other* people act a
certain way, why they've done the things they've done, continue
going from here to there, doing one thing, then another,
restless, always restless, going and going and going…and it's not
funny, it's not goddamn funny, it's not funny one bit, don't you
laugh, don't you even think it, don't you laugh one bit, you don't
know these people, you don't know what these people have
been through, how could you? how could you know what
certain people are thinking? you don't, don't think you do, you
don't know one bit, how could you?

and yet everybody's got something to say
but who knows what people are thinking?
smiling and smiling and stabbing you right in the back—
especially them people

them people would kill you in your sleep if you'd let them
and don't think they won't
don't you think they wouldn't kill you if they had the chance
because they will
you can't trust them people, no—

them people are not to be trusted
don't think you can—
them people are not your kind
you know what your people say about them people

them people will steal your underwear right from you
in the broad daylight if you let them
beat you down like a dog, like a goddamn animal
from head to toe—
leave you for dead
but how do you know?

how do you know how people are going to treat people
until it comes down to it?
you don't—
and that's what makes people crazy

one minute you can be going along and along and along,
minding your own business
and then the next, somebody's beating the hell out of you
and stealing your underwear
or threatening to kill you anyway

and then *of course* at other times there's all of you: *whites, blacks,
greens, reds, yellows, blues,* everybody—and I don't give a flying
fuck what on this goddamn earth those bastards try to tell you!

Are you listening to me?! I hope you're fucking listening to me!

…you see everybody's lying under the stars dreaming, curled up
like children and dreaming all sorts of things.
…and every once in a while *if you're lucky enough, who knows?!*
Arthur laughed—
…getting along like ordinary people!

ACT I: ORIGIN OF ACTION, PART 2

taking the long way
through the parking lot
to the front entrance
of the coffee shop
on the corner of mill plain
and the old post road
I heard him snicker
in my direction
then call over—
"friend, my friend" hey my friend it's me arthur
hey arthur it's arthur blunicki
as I ducked my head inside
and allowed the door
to close right behind me

looking back
through the frosted shop window
upon that cold damp winter day
I couldn't help but think
about that homeless man
and what he'd said to me
the day before

The History of the World

Love Poems and Other Stories
An American Debut
Vol. 1

J. Wilder-Hall

The light flashes across my desk and she jokes: In the mirror there's a face I don't recognize. I need to work but she doesn't understand. Always, I remind her, I'm in my father's garden, I'm rooted there. But she reads what I've written and disagrees with that too. Only human hands may carpenter obstacles to love, she says. As always life awakens to a world already beginning. Take, for example, the rose, she says. The rose your father planted when you were a little boy. And see him tenderly, my love. After all these years. Notice his arms opening up to you at last. The fractured vision of the heavenly man. Out there in the middle of these burgeoning fields. The two of you now flooded in sunlight. Now flooded by rain. Petals drifting everywhere against the sudden rush of cold.

Tenderly, She Arrives (From the Maryann Notebooks)
Flanagan Wallace, 1991

And Then There Were Two

A MUTUAL UNDERSTANDING

she sees me
as soon as i walk in

and goes straight
for the coffee machine

two creamers
two sugars

a saucer and spoon
i take my bar stool

the regular she says
all right i say

sets her pen to scribble
and walks away

     *

—You should hug him, she says.
—*Are you fucking crazy?*
—Tell him that you love him while there is still time…

AMERICA

the night before last
with(e radio turned on
wi)the water trickling
over dirty pots and pans
the noises oversuds hands
she started on it again—
about what happened
between frank and carolyn
our neighbors
from down the street
      standing by the kitchen sink
my love looked at me
with halfshut red eyes
then leaned her thin body
against mine
      "We'll be all right" I said
against the same old tired news
against the noise of kids yelling
across bedrooms—
      and pulled her closer
and closer still

this tired land
and loneliness all but fades

in these dark silhouettes
and lovers otherwise

A FEW HUNDRED METERS SOUTH OF THE TEL

And yet what will the gods say when these violent winds
have at long last passed
when the cherished words that are these words
have beautifully erupted

from the ashen mouth of the unborn babe's volcanic wings
when at long last my steady love
has become the smashed window
reckoned with at once opened eyes
founded on nothing more
perhaps than a ruse

and the untold difference between my longing
and her beating heart
is only but a measure

WILL YOU BE THERE?

*

Will you be there
When I'm all alone
When the lights go out
And there's no one at home
When darkness comes
And shatters the heart
When I'm crying like hell
When I'm falling apart

Will you pick me up
Will you lay me down
Will you hold back the waters
So I can be found
And we're lying in bed
And it's late at night
And you're dreaming of her
And it doesn't feel right

And I've screwed up again
And it's thirty years from now
And we've gone on too long
And we don't know how
So where do we go
And when did we lose it
When I'm no longer her
Will you shelter me through it

When I'm shaking like hell
When I'm threatening to die
Will you hold me so close
Look me right in the eyes
Will you kiss my cheeks
Will you warm my hands
Will you taste my lips
Etch my name in the sand

Will you carry my body
When I'm all alone
When the lights go out
And there's no one at home
When darkness comes
And shatters the heart
When I'm all out of tears
And you've fallen apart

ABOUT THE AUTHOR

J. Wilder-Hall was born in Bridgeport, Connecticut. He is the author of *The History of the World (Love Poems and Other Stories, An American Debut, Vol. 1)* and the short story collection *What Could We Have Possibly Known About Love Then?*

ALSO BY J. WILDER-HALL

What Could We Have Possibly Known About Love Then?

Navigating the precarious waters between heartbreak and loss, and written as the B-side to The History of the World, the short story collection What Could We Have Possibly Known About Love Then? picks up, in many respects, where THOTW leaves off—without any of the unnecessary delusions, but with a hopeful and resolute heart which pushes determinedly forward from the opening story "From Where We Live to Where We're Going" (which finds a thirty-year-old woman stranded on the highway in the driving wind and rain when her car's alternator fails: "Calling and calling practically everyone I knew. Where the hell was everyone?") toward its inevitable conclusion, "Epilogue: Equidistant to Center."

Showcasing the lives of hardscrabble Americans, extraordinary human beings caught suddenly in the middle of a life, these eleven wildly spiritual, heartbreaking, and at times raucously fun short stories (about fathers and sons, mothers and daughters, husbands, wives, neighbors, nurses, cops, robbers, mechanics, ex-lovers, and best friends, etc.) remind us time and time again of our very best selves and everything we have in our capacity to offer.

www.ingramcontent.com/pod-product-compliance
Lightning Source LLC
LaVergne TN
LVHW041156080426
835511LV00006B/625